Lucid

How to Start Lucid Dreaming
Even if You Never Remember Your Dreams

by Max Trance

maxtrance.com

DISCLAIMER

Use of this work and all material contained within it is entirely at your own risk. There are no guarantees of any kind around any of the material within this work, or anyone's use of it.

In particular, be aware that using the methods in this work may lead to hallucinations when you are awake, with all the consequences from that. While lucid dreaming is typically very safe, if you suffer from psychological issues you may want to check with your psychological professional before playing with lucid dreaming.

Nothing in this work is legal, financial, psychological, medical or any other kind of advice. Or to put it another way, the material in this work is for entertainment purposes only. And your entertainment is not guaranteed.

Now this should be abundantly clear from the above, but in case it is not: Neither you nor anyone else may take any kind of action against anyone associated with the creation, publication, distribution or sale of this work. Neither you nor anyone else may take action against any party associated with this work in any way. If you attempt to do so, you agree to be fully liable for everything including all costs and liabilities of all parties regardless of outcome. By way of example: if you take us to court, the only outcome is that you pay for everything on all sides, including any court-imposed liabilities and costs.

That said, the material presented in this work has worked effectively for me and other lucid dreamers. This does not mean that you will be successful in implementing it, and it does not mean that anyone other than you is responsible.

In using anything in this work, you assume full responsibility for any and all outcomes.

Table of Contents

Why lucid dream

Imagine a world so vivid that it is as real as the waking world. In this world, you can do anything you choose. You can be anyone or anything you choose. And you can travel to any place and any time.

One night you could be exploring the bottom of the ocean, seeing with crystal clarity where there is no light. The next night, you live out an entire lifetime as another being.

Perhaps you need to revise material for an exam. Or maybe you want to practice perfecting some move in the sport of your choosing.

When you lucid dream, there are no constraints or limits beyond your own imagination. With a little practice, the things that you discover and learn inside your lucid dreams can carry over into your waking world. This can be as simple as recalling what happened with clarity, or as complex as learning a new skill in your dreams and using it in the waking world.

As human beings, we live for around 80 years, and we tend to spend somewhere between a quarter and a third of that time sleeping. And even worse, most of us do not even recall our dreams clearly.

That's a lot of lost time. The good news is that with a little practice, you can learn to tame and control your dreams, and using the tools in this book it is possible to recall those dreams every bit as well as your waking life.

And it gets better. Have you ever had a dream that lasted for days, weeks, or longer, even though it occurred in a single night of sleeping? If you haven't, you have almost certainly heard of it.

You see, time works differently in dreams. Now I don't know how much time it is possible to experience in a single dream. I've never managed to guide someone past 50 years or so.

Even so, what would it mean for you if you could experience even one extra day every single night? And what would it be like if that day was perfect for you?

How much more happy and relaxed would you be if every second day that you experienced was spent doing anything you might desire? If you are competitive and like getting ahead, how much more quickly could you outpace the competition if you had twice as much time to train and study as they do? And if you're overworked, how much less stressed would you be if you were able to take a vacation after every day at work?

All of this and more has been achieved by people with lucid dreaming. And the best part is that it is a skill that anyone can learn.

The processes in this book have been designed to take you from never having remembered a dream, to having lucid dreams almost every night.

It will take a little effort on your part to get there, but the payoff is so huge that it is more than worth it. If you doubt this, just think about how much time, effort and money people spend trying to keep themselves from dying so that they can live a handful of years longer. How much time would you invest if you were certain it would get you another decade of life?

When you become an exceptional lucid dreamer, the possibility opens up to extend your effective perceived life by countless lifetimes, lived out in dreams that are every bit as real to you as the reality you're in as you're reading this right now.

And all that is required for most people to become exceptional is a little effort and consistent deliberate practice.

What is lucid dreaming

In its simplest form, lucid dreaming is exactly what it sounds like: you have dreams in which you are fully conscious and aware. Most lucid dreamers choose to take it further, and actively shape their dreams so that they can experience anything they might desire.

The huge advantage of this is that our brains already create these dream realities inside our minds just about every time we sleep. So we already have the base framework that we need to get started.

This means that if we want to experience lucid dreams, there is a very short list of skills we need to acquire.

First, we need a way to recall our dreams. If we don't have this, then all the lucidity in the world won't help, because it would be as though the events in our dreams never happened as soon as we wake up. This part is quite easy, even if you've never recalled your dreams before. In this book, I share the technique that I used to quickly and easily go from recalling maybe one dream a year, to recalling one or more dreams in vivid detail every single night.

Second, we need a way to become conscious within those dreams. For most people, this is the hard part. Luckily, once you know a little about how the mind works, this too can become almost effortless.

Third, we need a way to take control of our dreams. In a lot of ways, this is the easiest part. If we don't do this, we can end up conscious and aware, but unable to manipulate our dreams very much. This would make them much like the waking world. Which is often not a bad thing in itself, but why settle for a clone of reality when you could have everything you can imagine?

That's really the only skills we need in order to learn to lucid dream, and we're going to cover how to acquire each of them later on in this book.

Now, it will aid us immensely in having lucid dreams if we understand just a little about how the mind works. It's quite a bit different to how most people imagine, because our experience of our own minds is from the inside.

So before we get into exactly how to lucid dream, I'm going to quickly cover off some things.

There are many models of how the mind works. We hypnotists tend to use a model where we think of the mind as being composed of a conscious part and an unconscious part, and this model is to a large extent useful.

If you think about it, the human brain is essentially a vast neural network with the information accumulated over a lifetime of experiences stored in more than a quadrillion connections between neurons. Not only that, but those connections are not simple on-off switches. Instead, they are analog data stores with an effectively infinite range of values.

(As an aside to my fellow physicists and mathematicians: Ok so it's not really infinite. If you like, feel free to estimate the number of atoms in an average neural connection and compute the number of possible combinations and configurations. It's really, really big. Then add on the effects of the myelin wrapper and it gets even bigger.)

This entire system is constantly changing. We perceive time on a scale of seconds, because it takes a few milliseconds for one of these connections to reshape itself within our brains.

Data continuously flows into the system from a huge array of sources. We receive it from sensors all over and inside our bodies. These include the regular five senses of sight, sound, smell, taste, and touch, along with numerous other senses that are not usually talked about outside of fields where they are studied, including such things as the position of every part of our body that we can move, tension, hunger, multiple types of pain, temperature, and a whole host of others.

Suffice it to say that there are billions of pieces of information flowing into our minds from our environments and from our bodies all the time.

A lot of these pieces of information are relatively stable. For example, the temperature of various parts of our bodies does not change very much unless we do something to cause it to. Right now as I am writing this, I am sitting in a kitchen and there is a stove in my field of vision... that image is completely stable for the time being.

At the same time, a lot of the data changes constantly. Right now, I can hear cicadas and birds chirping outside. The pressure on my fingertips is continually changing as I type. And I can feel the temperature in my palms fluctuating as I raise and lower my hands.

On top of all of that, we also have other information constantly coming in. You see, our thoughts never really stop. We're constantly thinking about stuff. And those thoughts form another data source for our minds.

Yep. Our minds are shaped not only by our environment, but also by our minds.

When information flows into our minds, our neural network is reshaped. Our brains are organized in such a way that they effectively perform an operation known as chunking. This is where information flows in, and the response of our neural network creates abstract structures inside our minds known as chunks. In simple terms, a chunk is the representation of an object or concept inside our minds.

So for example, right now there is that stove in my field of vision. When I look at it, the information goes into my mind and combines with the information about every other stove I've ever experienced, along with the environments around them, and other stove-like objects and associated thoughts. When I look at the screen, the stove is still in my field of vision, but I'm not really paying attention to it, or even aware of its existence to any great degree.

With all that data flowing into our minds, you might ask just how much of it can we be aware of at once. This is a question that has been studied, and it turns out that the answer is just four things.

Now, because our brains chunk information so quickly, if we run an experiment, we typically find that most people can actually keep track of between 5 and 9 things at once. With a little training they can get as high as 11.

That's not a lot when you consider the billions of pieces of information constantly flowing in and shaping our minds.

We hypnotists typically deal with this by considering all the stuff we're not thinking about right now to be the unconscious mind, and that tiny handful of things we are thinking about as being the conscious mind.

There are a few other models out there, and they all come back to the same thing: as human beings, at any point in time we are only capable of paying attention to the tiniest part of our current experience, and that current experience includes any thoughts we may be having.

If you are spiritual or religious, feel free to include that as we go along. I won't be covering those topics much in this book because even though they are an important part of lucid dreaming for many people, they are not required to make it work. Not only that, but if I were to try to cover them, many people with differing perspectives would complain, and this book would end up being many, many thousands of pages long. There are simply too many different ways of doing them and that's not what this book is about.

Suffice it to say that if religion or spirituality, or both, are important to you, you will almost certainly enhance your experience of lucid dreaming by taking a few moments to incorporate them into it. And the person who best knows how to do that is you.

So how does all of this tie into lucid dreaming?

Well, when we fall asleep, we lose most of the data feed from the outside world. It's typically dark and our eyes are closed, so we lose the visual feed. We're generally lying somewhere comfortable and safe and warm, so we lose the kinesthetic feed. We're not eating anything, so we lose the taste feed. We don't usually move much, so our awareness of temperature and position tends to fall even further.

I'm sure you get the idea.

But what don't stop are our thoughts. They can't stop because if they did, we would be dead. Our thoughts shift up and down.

Sometimes they're quiet and we drift peacefully along into ever deeper sleep. Other times they become active and approach the levels that they are at when we're awake.

We tend to think of ourselves as being either awake or asleep, but in reality, we exist in a continuum ranging from wide awake, alert and fully in the moment, all the way down to deep sleep, or even coma.

When we sleep, we run through a largely automated process where over the course of 90 minutes or so we start off in relatively light sleep, drift down to deep sleep, drift back up to light sleep, then we dream for a bit. This cycle repeats multiple times every night.

By the way, if you've ever woken up feeling groggy and unrested despite apparently sleeping the entire night, this often happens because we wake up at the wrong point in the sleep cycle. When we wake up at the end of a sleep cycle, we generally feel well rested. And the easiest way to wake up at the right point in our sleep cycle is to allow it to happen naturally. This is why alarm clocks are a really bad idea.

Is lucid dreaming dangerous?

Now, before we get into how to create a lucid dream so that you can start having them, it is important that we go over a few things that can happen so that you don't freak out, or worse, act out your dreams in real life, if they happen to you.

For what I hope are obvious reasons, there could be unfortunate consequences if we were to act out in real life everything that can happen in our imagination. So when we dream, our bodies need some way of not acting out the activities in those dreams. Luckily, there is a handy mechanism built into our brains that essentially shuts down our ability to move most of our muscles.

Known as sleep paralysis, this can be a scary thing to experience if you wake up while it is still in effect. Sleep paralysis is a natural process that happens when we dream. It is there to keep us, and those around us, safe. I mention it here because when you start working with creating lucidity in your dreams, the possibility increases that you will wake up at a point where your sleep paralysis is still running.

There are various techniques to overcome sleep paralysis, and for our purposes here, it is enough to know that it is a completely safe and natural process, and that if you experience it when you wake up, the worst that can happen is that you fall asleep again.

Even before I knew how to overcome sleep paralysis, it never lasted for more than 15 minutes after waking, so all you really have to do is wait for a bit and think about something else. If nothing else, it is a wonderful opportunity to start planning your day.

Just make sure you don't focus your attention on the sleep paralysis itself. This is the one thing that can cause it to continue indefinitely.

Next up we have hallucinations. A lot of people have the belief that hallucinations only happen when something is wrong (such as not enough sleep, too many drugs, and so on). This is far from the truth.

In reality, our experience of the world is an hallucination that plays out on what is effectively a multi-sensory screen inside our mind.

When we are awake, this hallucination is mostly generated by information flowing in from the outside world. But there is also the constant stream of information from our thoughts.

Hallucinations tend to take the form of a constructed experience in any or all of our senses. When you hallucinate, you might experience hearing a sound that isn't there, or feeling a touch even when nothing is in contact with your skin.

We can also experience negative hallucinations, which is where we do not experience something that is there. If you've ever been totally absorbed in a good book or movie, you've probably experienced everything falling away from your awareness other than the story you were following. This is just one of many types of negative hallucinations.

Now, depending on your level of skill at hallucinating, you may even be able to experience visual hallucinations.

To give you an idea of the range of experience possible, I have personally been able to experience auditory hallucinations for my entire life, to the extent that I never bother to play music because there is a constant soundtrack in my mind that sounds just like the real thing. In contrast, I did not experience a visual hallucination until I was in my late teens, and even then, only with my eyes closed. It was not until my mid 30s that I managed a visual hallucination with my eyes open. And it was not until my mid 40s that I was finally able to experience a kinesthetic hallucination.

Yep. I am old.

Other people find it effortless to have visual hallucinations, but struggle with auditory or kinesthetic. Any combination is possible and all of them can be learnt. And because our western education system does not cover these things, we typically have no baseline to measure ourselves against, so there isn't really any way to notice where we are on the scale other than by putting ourselves through the experiences.

By the same token, I have worked with people who can quite easily experience full sensory hallucinations with nothing more than some simple hypnosis.

The reason that it is important to know this is that when we start to play with things like lucid dreaming, we are training our minds to experience some part of our thoughts as reality. This can have flow-on effects. If you have never experienced an hallucination before, or if you are like most people and have experienced them but didn't realize they were hallucinations, you could potentially end up in a dangerous situation.

The good news is that when you learn to lucid dream, at the same time you will be learning how to control your hallucinations, since both are caused by the same mental processes. I am of the opinion that this is much better than the position that most people find themselves in where not only can they not tell that something is an hallucination, they also cannot do anything to turn it off.

In short, if you don't learn to lucid dream, you are constantly at risk of believing that things are real when they are actually constructs inside your mind. Imagine what could happen if you were to hallucinate while driving. It would be bad, right? Once you know how to control your dreams, and by extension, any hallucinations you might experience, this risk can be greatly diminished.

Now, just as we can hallucinate, which is essentially nothing more than a form of dreaming while fully awake, we can also do the opposite. That is, it is possible to dream that you have woken up when you are still sound asleep. The only real consequence of this one is that if you think you're awake when you are still asleep, you're wasting a dream that you could be shaping in any way you might choose!

As you might be able to guess by now, we're never really fully asleep or fully awake. It is more the case that we exist on a spectrum of consciousness in which our state changes from moment to moment.

You may have heard of other processes such as meditation, mindfulness and hypnosis and be wondering how these relate to lucid dreaming. Since all of these deal with the mind, it would not be a lie to say that they are all different aspects of the same thing. Specifically, each is a different means of controlling the behavior of our minds.

In meditation, we are effectively training ourselves to focus deeply and to view things from all possible perspectives. When we do this, it strengthens the abilities of our minds in areas such as creativity.

Mindfulness is more about being fully present in the moment and paying attention to what's going on. This enhances our perceptions of the things around us and inside us. It's also a key factor in lucidity within dreaming. If you want to be lucid in your dreams, it is much easier if you can already do it in your waking state.

In contrast, even though it uses similar techniques, self-hypnosis is more about accessing the largest part of our mind that we don't normally have access to and making changes to overcome whatever challenges we may be facing.

And hypnosis itself is a state in which we bypass the conscious interference (that's our logical mind trying to mess things up) in order to make deep changes. Or just to have some fun.

As you can imagine, each of these is heavily intertwined with the others. Many processes that hypnotists use to guide subjects into hypnosis are exactly the same as those used by meditators and by those who are practicing being mindful.

Which brings us to the final point in this chapter. If you ask most people, they will tell you that they can easily tell the difference between something that is imagined and something that is real.

This is sort of true, and sort of not true.

It is true that our conscious, logical minds can generally make this distinction quite easily. And this is the part of us that we are most aware of. That's kinda what conscious means.

However, our unconscious minds (that's everything we're not aware of right now) don't work that way at all. Instead, the unconscious part of our mind simply processes information and associates stuff with other stuff. For the most part, it cannot tell the difference at all between something that is real and something that is imagined.

As luck would have it, when we pay attention to what's going on around us, we can effectively block a lot of things from making their way into our mind. If we don't pay attention, no such filter exists.

I'm vastly oversimplifying here, but it is helpful to appreciate that we have this tiny part of our mind that can tell us what is highly likely to be real, and this huge part of our mind that we can't really see at all that assumes that everything is real regardless of whether it is real or we're just imagining it.

As you can imagine, this is good news if we want to exploit our lucid dreams for studying and practicing new skills!

How to lucid dream

So how exactly do we have a lucid dream? And how do we remember our dreams so that we even know it's happened?

Let's begin with what a dream is. At its simplest, a dream is created when our minds play out the events of our lives while we sleep. Because of the way that neural networks work, the end result is often nothing at all like anything from our lives. This has enormous benefits for us, since it means that we can do literally anything we choose inside our dreams once we've learnt to control them.

You should also feel free to add in any spiritual significance that is appropriate for your particular beliefs. I can't do that, because I don't know you, and everyone is different.

I've split this chapter up into sections covering each component typically required to consistently experience lucid dreams. This is so that after you've read it once, you can easily find whatever skill you are working on for reference in the future.

How our minds work

Now, an interesting thing about our minds is that they have a tendency to run in loops. When we think about something, we tend to end up thinking more about the same thing. This happens because our minds are constantly being fed data not only from the outside, but also from our own thoughts.

If you know how to code, you can quickly discover not only why this happens, but also that it is guaranteed to happen inside a neural network that feeds into itself.

You see, the way our brains (and other neural networks) work is that when two neurons are stimulated at the same time, they tend to become connected. The end result of this is that when we experience multiple things at the same time, they end up linked inside our minds. Once that happens, thinking about our experience will tend to strengthen those links. This is why we can mentally revise our notes after we've been studying, and find that our memory of what we've been learning improves.

Also, bear in mind that this happens at all scales. Right now I am sitting at a beach and a seagull just landed in front of me. I can look at its head and notice that it has an orange beak with a close-to-black tip.

Now, inside my eyes, there are millions of receptors that are essentially the equivalent of pixels on a screen. A CCD camera is an even better analogy, but screens are easier for most people to visualize.

There are probably hundreds, if not thousands of receptors that pick up that orange coloring, and feed it into my neural network. These all combine together with all previous representations of that shade of orange, along with the more specific representation of seagulls, and the broader representations of birds, animals, and things. And a whole lot more. This happens constantly at all scales. As my mind constructs an image of a beak, it is simultaneously making images of a seagull and the beach beyond it and linking all of it together and with my past experiences.

This constant linking and association of stuff with other similar stuff inside our minds is also why it's really easy to remember happy memories when we're happy, and difficult to remember the sad ones. And why we find it difficult to remember happy memories when we're sad.

Not only that, but when things are foremost in our mind, it is much easier for us to access them. You can probably remember exactly what you had for breakfast this morning, but most people would struggle to recall what they had for breakfast on the eighth Tuesday in 2007.

When we put all of this together we end up with some interesting things going on.

First and foremost, if we want to have things happen in our dreams, we have a much greater chance of that if we repeatedly practice thinking about them throughout the day.

How to remember

There are essentially two things that drive our ability to remember stuff. As you probably noticed in school, when we repeat things a lot of times, they tend to stick in our minds. This is how rote learning works. If you feel so inclined, you can play around with neural network software and you will very quickly discover that the more you reinforce some data by repeatedly playing it into the neural network, the stronger the associated connections become.

The other way is a little more subtle. We all have things that have happened to us throughout our lives that we recall with crystal clarity despite there being no repetition. If you think back over them for a moment, you'll notice a common theme. Every single time, there was a strong emotion associated with it. This told your brain that it was important.

As it turns out, negative emotions are a lot more effective at causing us to recall things than are positive emotions.

The reason for this is a lot more straightforward than it might first appear. If you think back to our distant ancestors in prehistoric times, it didn't matter very much if they forgot things like having a good laugh around the fire with their friends. But it mattered quite a lot if they forgot that being eaten by lions is bad. As thousands of years passed, the people who forgot such things died out as they were eaten before they had children to whom to pass on their forgetfulness.

Fast forward to the 21st century, and we find that there are two things that we can all draw on to help us to make memories. The first is repetition, and the second is having a strong emotion when we are forming the memory. The stronger we can make the emotion, the fewer times we have to repeat something before we can reliably remember it.

As I mentioned, negative emotions tend to be more effective than positive emotions in this regard. This is not a reason to use negative emotions to help us remember. It is more the case that we want to make sure that the positive emotions we feel when forming memories are somewhat bigger than the negative ones we experience throughout our day to day lives. If we don't do this, we can end up with our dreams saturated with negativity. I don't know about you, but I prefer to avoid nightmares!

In the context of making sure the footprint in our mind of the positive emotions is bigger than that of the negative ones, bigger can be longer lasting and it can be stronger. Usually it is some combination of both.

How big this is will be different for everyone. All I can suggest around this is that you experiment, have fun, and discover what happens for you.

So why do I mention all of this? We'll come to that a little later on when we get up to reality checks and anchoring. For now, just feel a strong sense of pride and achievement, smugness even, or any other positive emotion that works for you, as you think about how you now know the two ways you can make any memory stick. Either you repeat it, like I've done just now, or you generate a massive emotion to tell your brain that it's important.

The end result of everything we've covered so far is that our dreams tend to reflect our reality over the preceding days, weeks and even years. And the more recent something is, the more it tends to impact our dreams.

The importance of planning

Have you ever had the experience of going to the supermarket to buy just one thing, and coming away with a load of groceries, only to get home and realize that you bought everything but the one thing you went there to buy? I know that I have. And if you haven't, you almost certainly know people who have done this.

We go there with that one intention and we try to stay focused on it. But our conscious minds can only hang on to four things at once. As soon as we exceed that, unless we have some kind of process to follow, our success is largely down to luck. There are easy ways to work around this. For example, we can make a shopping list. We can also use techniques such as the *method of loci* to give us an easy way back to that memory.

If you're not familiar with it, at its core the method of loci works by associating something we want to remember with something we can easily remember. For example, you can probably close your eyes right now and get a sense of where everything in your house is located. You can probably do this for many of the places that you've ever lived in.

So one way of using the method of loci might be that you see a room in your house clearly, notice a handful of locations in that room, and then mentally place one thing that you want to recall in each of those locations. Naturally you'll need to either repeat this a few times, or generate a strong emotion if you want it to actually work.

Then when you want to remember the specific item, all you have to do is think about that location in your house, which is very easy for most people to do, and the item you wanted to remember will generally pop into your mind right away.

Understanding this point is one of the keys to achieving lucidity in your dreams.

Now since we know that our dreams will tend to reflect our recent reality, this gives us a baseline to start to shape them. While it is possible to change the shape of our dreams from the inside, if we want to be effective, it is generally a good idea to get as close as possible to what we want before we even start.

Think about it: if we hop in our car and drive somewhere random, we probably won't end up in the next city. But if we decide beforehand that we are going to drive to the next city, we will usually get there.

If we want to be exploring prehistoric times in our dreams, it is not going to help us get there if we spend the time right before we fall asleep thinking about the dramas at the office, catching up on the news, or even planning what we're going to be doing tomorrow. On the other hand, it will help us immensely if we spend that time thinking about what those prehistoric times must have been like, what kinds of creatures were around, and so on.

When we intentionally shape our thoughts right before we sleep, we are much more likely to experience dreams that involve those thoughts in some way.

What you can do inside your dreams

Before we come to dream planning, there is one more topic that we need to cover. And that topic is what exactly can we do in our dreams.

The answer to this one is straightforward. Inside our dreams, we can do literally anything we can imagine. The laws of physics do not apply. The laws of reality do not apply. Math and logic can work differently in any way you might choose. With enough practice, even the people in your dreams can react in ways that you choose. They are a part of you after all. And if you want to spend a dream experiencing life as an alien amoeba floating through space in a distant galaxy, there is nothing standing in your way other than your willingness to go there inside your mind.

There are two broad categories that our dreams can fall into, and just like real life, it is possible for dreams to have elements from both.

First, we can have dreams where we explore and try out new things.

It could be that we want to visit dinosaurs, flying around on the back of a pterodactyl, or spend time with vampires. Perhaps you're like me and just want to be somewhere warm and relaxing with a gentle breeze. Or you might want to experience somewhere entirely different... an alien planet, the bottom of the ocean, or perhaps a tranquil monastery... any place and any time is available to you.

Not only that, but in your dreams you can become not only other people and experience the dream world through their eyes, you can also become other creatures or beings. Maybe you'd like to be a kitten, playfully exploring a garden for the first time. If you really want to, you can even become inanimate objects, such as rocks, and experience the world in that way. Or perhaps you'd like to experience what it's like to be a star powering your own solar system.

The options are endless, and once you have learnt to become lucid in your dreams, the only limit is your imagination.

Second, we can have dreams where we study and practice new skills.

This one is slightly different, because we do need some material to work on before we start to dream.

I've heard numerous lucid dreamers make claims such as *books in dreams do not have words* or *the words inside books in dreams change when you look away*.

All I can say about that is that if you have not taken the time to first read the book you want to study in your dreams, it should not come as a surprise if it is unstable. When I choose to study in my dreams, the very first thing I do is make sure that I've covered the material while awake. Otherwise my brain has nothing to go on. And I've found that when I do this, dream books are every bit as stable as books out in the waking world.

It is the same with anything else you want to study or practice inside your dreams. Your mind needs something to grasp onto first. If you want to practice that new golf swing, you first have to know what it's like. It could be that it is enough for you to look at a few pictures, but for most people we probably have to grab a club and try to swing it a few times before we dream.

Once we do this, our mind knows broadly how the specific thing works, and we're in a good place to have dreams around it.

So how do we make it happen?

Well the very first step is to consciously decide what it is that we are going to dream about tonight. We do this while we are still awake.

As a rule, the more detail we put into our dream plans, the more likely we are to have those dreams.

An important part of learning to lucid dream is measuring what happens every time you dream. The easiest way to do this is usually to write everything down. You can do this with a dream journal, a regular diary, or even an app on your phone. If you'd like to be guided through the process, I've put together a dream planner and journal that can be purchased wherever you bought this book:

Lucid Dreaming Planner and Journal by Max Trance

If I can get the colors right, it will even have a cover photo of the beach I was sitting at when I mentioned the seagull.

Now you might be wondering if you really need to write out your plan and a journal of what happens in your dreams, and the answer is yes, you do.

If you think about it, we have countless thoughts every day and we forget most of them as soon as we have them. The unconscious part of our minds doesn't really have any way to tell which ones are important beyond being repeated a lot and having strong emotions attached, so what do you think is likely to win and make it into your dreams if all you do is think about it: the dream you spent five minutes planning, or the ten hours or more that you spent at work?

Similarly, when we write things into a document on our phone or computer... well... for most of us, every day we type countless meaningless things on one or both of these types of devices. And this tells our brain that stuff we write on an electronic device is not important.

On the other hand, these days most people almost never write things out by hand. And when we do, it tends to be only for things that are important to us. Our unconscious mind can learn quickly, and so it will automatically assume that if something is written out by hand, it must be important.

The practical upshot is this: If you want to get the best possible results, write out your dream plans by hand.

For the same reason, you will probably get better results if you buy a specific lucid dreaming planner and journal than if you just use sheets of paper from your printer. In essence, the act of buying the lucid dreaming planner and journal for a specific purpose tells your unconscious mind that it must be important.

The underlying rule is that the more you can tell your unconscious mind that something is important, the more likely it is that your unconscious mind will pay attention and actually do what you want it to.

That said, any form of writing is better than just thinking about it. So if you don't have a dream planner yet, grab a diary (or a sheet of paper from your printer) and a pen and take a few moments to answer these questions every time you are planning your dreams:

What is the date today?

What time will I go to bed?

Is there anything going on emotionally or otherwise that could mess with my sleep?

How much caffeine did I consume today?

How much alcohol did I consume today?

What medications did I consume today?

What goal will I set for my dream tonight?

What am I going to dream about tonight?

I have found that caffeine does not have a huge impact on my ability to dream or to become lucid inside those dreams. But I also do not tend to drink coffee after lunchtime and rarely have more than two cups a day.

I've heard from others that caffeine does have a disruptive effect on dreaming, so you'll have to test it yourself if caffeine is important to you.

In contrast, even two standard drinks of alcohol are enough to significantly inhibit my dreams. If you live somewhere where other drugs are legal, you will probably find the same thing with them. It tends to be a good idea to avoid substances that interfere with the usual working of your brain if you want to experience vivid dreams.

The exception to this rule is probably ayahuasca. Ayahuasca is illegal where I live, so I have not tried it myself, but I have heard from multiple people that it can result in some very interesting effects. If you live somewhere where this is legal, I strongly encourage you to not try it without suitable oversight from an expert. There are numerous stories out in the world about people having psychotic breaks, or even dying, from using that particular drug.

On the other hand, shamans have apparently used ayahuasca for thousands of years to enhance their own lucid dreaming experiences, so it would be an oversight to not include at least a mention of it here.

Getting back to the questions though... the purpose of all of these questions is to enable you to track the effects that each thing has on your ability to dream.

For example, if you notice that you never recall your dreams after having four cups of coffee the day before, you will have the opportunity to decide whether coffee or your dreams are more important.

When you are choosing the goal of your dream, this should be the thing you want to achieve. Just as with driving to another city, we are unlikely to achieve a goal if we don't know what it is. It can be anything at all: climbing Mount Everest, visiting Ancient Rome, practicing our knitting technique, or anything else you like. We do need to set it though since without a goal we won't be able to measure whether we achieved it the following morning.

Which brings us to the final question: what am I going to dream about tonight. With this one the trick is balance. You don't want to write too little, because your brain won't think it is important. You also don't want to write too much, because that might confine your dreams. Also, when people have to spend a lot of time planning to do something like dreaming, it becomes very easy to simply not do the planning at all.

I suggest that the optimal amount of planning time to start with is perhaps a few minutes. Think about the broad shape you would like your dreams to take on. An example might look like:

Tonight I am going to dream that I am flying around a prehistoric island on the back of a pterodactyl. There is a volcano on the island and lava is bubbling up inside the crater, but not spilling over the sides. The island is covered in trees and is surrounded by gorgeous golden sand beaches. I can see tyrannosauruses and brontosauruses roaming around the island and I am going to ride the back of one of them after landing the pterodactyl. The sky is a brilliant blue and there are some fluffy white clouds in the sky.

By going to this level of detail, we decide on what the basic structure looks like, while leaving enough space for us to explore and discover new things. Maybe the volcano will erupt. Perhaps we'll find a hut where we can sleep. It could be that we find a hammock high up in some trees and spend some time lying in the sun looking out at the ocean and the blue sky. Or anything else at all.

Notice that in the paragraph above where I describe a dream, it is written in the present tense. It's not in the future. It's not in the past. It's not written as a possibility. Instead it is something that is happening now. This is important because it makes it slightly more real for our minds. To see this, run each of these paragraphs through your mind, and notice which one feels more real and more compelling:

First, our original paragraph:

Tonight I am going to dream that I am flying around a prehistoric island on the back of a pterodactyl. There is a volcano on the island and lava is bubbling up inside the crater, but not spilling over the sides. The island is covered in trees and is surrounded by gorgeous golden sand beaches. I can see some tyrannosauruses and brontosauruses roaming around the island and I am going to ride the back of one of them after landing the pterodactyl. The sky is a brilliant blue and there are some fluffy white clouds in the sky.

And now let's make it a bit more wishy-washy:

Tonight it would be kinda nice if I had a dream. In that dream I might fly around a prehistoric island somehow. There could be a volcano and some trees, maybe even a beach and some random dinosaurs.

Run each of those paragraphs through your mind, and notice the difference.

The other thing that it is important to realize is that there are no hard and fast rules here. You will need to experiment to work out what is the optimal amount for you to write, and what is the optimal level of detail. When you plan your dreams by writing them out beforehand, there is also the added bonus that afterwards you can measure the results. This means that over time you can figure out what works for you and what doesn't.

After you've written out your dream plan, take a few moments to imagine what that will feel like, what the colours will be like, what kinds of sounds and smells there will be. The more details you can add in with your imagination before you dream, the more likely you will be to experience those details in your dream. Ideally you want to fall asleep daydreaming about what it will be like to experience that dream that you've planned.

Time distortion

Have you heard the expression *a watched pot never boils*? If you haven't, next time you have the opportunity, fill a pot with some cold water, place it on the stove, turn on the element, start a stopwatch, and do nothing but wait for it to boil. In particular, make sure you do not talk to anyone, read things on your phone, look at the stopwatch, or do anything else to engage yourself.

Now, depending on the starting temperature of the water, atmospheric pressure, humidity, the initial volume of water, and the rate at which thermal energy is transferred into the water, it could take a long time or a short time. If you've filled a small pot with cold water, it's probably going to boil in less than ten minutes.

So you run the experiment. Fill the pot and wait for it to boil. Do not do anything else while you wait.

It feels like a really long time, right? And yet, when you look at the stopwatch afterwards, it was clearly only a few minutes.

The truth is that our perception of time is not constant. There are activities we can do where time seems to drag on forever, and there are activities where it seems to be gone in the blink of an eye.

And the worst part is that unless you know how to control it, by default it is the boring, uninteresting activities that we don't want to be doing that seem to take the longest. And it is the fun, exciting ones where we are in a state of flow that seem to disappear in the blink of an eye.

This is good news when it comes to dreaming.

You see, our minds know how to adjust how much time we perceive. That's why we get those effects when we're waiting for something, or when we're having fun. It's just that most people don't know how to do it consciously.

Conveniently, it is our unconscious mind that drives this phenomenon. And it is our unconscious mind that drives our dreams.

The end result of this is that if we want to experience a lot of time in our dreams, quite often all we have to do is decide how long we will be there when we are planning.

So for example, we might start our plan with a statement like:

In my dream tonight I will spend an entire day sailing around Bermuda on a 45 foot sailboat.

Then we add in the details about how much time we are going to spend doing each activity that day. When we do this, our unconscious mind will generally automatically make us experience enough time to fit it all in.

In hypnosis, we have other ways to deliberately expand the amount of time that you perceive. I'm not going to go into those here because with dreams it is typically enough to set the intention into your plan.

If you're interested in going further with time distortion, the process that I cover in my book **The Self-Hypnosis Formula** is specifically designed to cause significant amounts of time distortion.

Your dream lab

Suppose that you want to learn something in your dream. Perhaps you want to come up with creative solutions to a problem you've been trying to solve. Or maybe you want to practice a physical skill.

The way that you do this is by designing what I refer to as a dream lab inside your plan.

Even though I've labelled it as a lab, this is mostly because I happen to be a scientist. You can label your lab as anything that suits you.

If you're into a sport, it's probably more useful to you to make it into an appropriate location for practicing your sport.

And if it is some kind of craft that you're wanting to practice, you'll want to make it a location where you can practice that craft.

The key is that you want to design your lab to suit the task at hand.

Since I am a physicist and a hypnotist, my dream lab is (naturally) set in an ancient stone castle with lab benches, bubbling concoctions with tubing, conical flasks and tesla coils. It also has all manner of technological devices, along with the ability to summon pretty much any scientist from history. And from the future.

To create your own dream lab, all you do is decide what it's for, then make a plan for it.

First, decide what your dream lab is for. This can be anything at all. By way of example, if you want to practice your golf swings, it could be a driving range. Or it could be a full golf course with a multitude of different holes. You get to choose. And it is not even set in stone, because you can change it any time you might choose to in the future.

If you are artistic, feel free to draw out what it will look like on a blank piece of paper.

Then write out a plan:

When I dream tonight I will be in my new woodworking shop. It is a large room with a lathe, drill press, and a sturdy workbench. Around the walls, I can see each of my tools hanging ready to go. My tools are conveniently grouped to make them easy to find so that most of the time all I have to do is look up and I find the tool I am looking for. Today I am practicing using the lathe on a particularly difficult piece of jarrah, paying close attention to how the wood responds every time I cut into it. I practice with my lathe for a full 12 hours until I get it just right. When I come back to this room in the future, I refer to it as my woodworking shop.

I'm sure you get the idea. In this particular case, you would need to have had at least some experience with working on jarrah with a lathe. Otherwise your brain won't have anything to latch onto and will just make up random crap. While this is entertaining for many dreams, it is not useful when we want to practice a skill.

The last sentence in the plan is there to solidify a label for our dream lab. When we give names to our dream environments, it creates a structure inside our mind which makes it easier to come back to the same place in the future. In the case of a dream lab, this is something that we would like to have happen.

That way, when we want to return to our woodworking shop in the future, all we have to do is reference it at the start of our dream plan for that night:

When I dream tonight I am in my woodworking shop.

Stuff that won't work

I'm going to make a prediction. When you talk with other lucid dreamers, it won't be long before you start to run into claims that may seem inconsistent with things you've experienced.

The key with all of it is to ask yourself if something actually makes sense.

I'll give you a couple of examples that have come up recently.

First, as I already mentioned, I've heard more than a few people claim that you cannot read books inside your dreams. I've even heard them claim that you can use this as a test that you are dreaming.

In reality, so long as a copy of the book is inside your mind, there is no reason at all why you can't read it in a dream. What you cannot do is read a book that you've never read.

In this case, all you have to do is ask yourself whether the information is already in your mind in some way. If you have experienced that information, then in some form, it is going to be there.

For example, in the case of a book: if you have read the book, its contents will largely be inside your unconscious mind somewhere.

Similarly, if you have not read the book in question, no amount of dreaming is going to miraculously create a clone of it. I suspect that this is where the idea that you cannot read a book in your dreams comes from.

The reason this is important is that as you pursue more lucid dreams, you will almost certainly absorb ideas from others. If someone tells you that you can tell that you are dreaming because dream books are always unstable, or have no words... well... you're probably going to conclude that you are awake when you are actually dreaming.

Similarly, I've heard claims that you can tell that you are dreaming by flicking a light switch and noticing that it doesn't work. All I can say about this is that light switches and other technological devices always work in my dreams. And they don't always work in the waking world. This is a sign of a not-good test.

Once again, the test is simple: ask yourself whether the thing you are doing is something that you have experienced while awake.

If it is, then your mind knows what should happen and you can choose whether or not to implement that behavior in your dreams.

Which brings us nicely to the topic of reality checks.

Reality checks

When we dream, it can seem completely real to us, so if we want to manipulate that dream we need a means to determine that we are dreaming.

We do this with a reality check.

At its simplest, a reality check is nothing more than a test we can conduct both in the waking world and in our dreams that can behave differently in our dreams.

The main issue with a reality check is being able to remember to do it in your dream so that you can discover you are dreaming.

If you think back to earlier in this book, you will recall that our dreams are more likely to include things that we experience in the lead-up to sleeping, and that we experience throughout the day immediately before.

Conveniently, we can use this to make it likely that we will actually perform reality checks in our dreams.

In order to make this happen, first we have to choose something that we can use as a reality check. There is almost infinite variety here, so I suggest starting off with something simple, such as pushing a finger into your palm and intending for it to go all the way through. Whatever it is that you choose, make sure that it is something that won't cause you or anyone else an injury when you do it while awake.

It is vitally important that you choose something that is impossible in the waking world for your reality check.

Once you've selected something to do, you want to build the habit of doing that thing repeatedly throughout the day. There are a couple of ways to do this.

If your day is very structured, you may be able to perform your reality check at the start or end of specific activities throughout the day. For example, if you have meetings all day every day, you could make it into a ritual for the start of every meeting. The downside to this is that you'll probably only do a reality check in your dreams when you dream of a meeting.

If your day is less structured, you may have to set an alarm to remind you. Just make sure you don't set an alarm that will go off while you are sleeping.

Then all you do is perform your reality check, and notice what happens. When we do this enough, what tends to happen is that we start performing our reality checks automatically.

If you think back to when we talked about how memory works earlier, it is all by association. The central idea with reality checks is twofold. First, we want to be doing them habitually so that we habitually do them in our dreams. And second, we want them associated with as many things that we might dream about as possible, so that when we dream about those things, we automatically perform a reality check.

Once we are performing our reality checks automatically in the waking world, there is a very good chance that we will continue to do them in our dreams.

Next, when you perform your reality check in your dream, and it actually works, you will know you are dreaming. This is your sign to wake up inside your dream, become lucid, and start to utilize your dream in any way you might choose.

I'll give you an example to make this concrete. Last night, I wrote out my dream plan as usual, and then found myself thinking about this book that you're reading right now. I drifted off to sleep and woke up the next day.

Without really thinking about it much, I got up and eventually found myself writing on my computer.

Now as you might imagine since I've written a book on it, I've been lucid dreaming for years. As a result of this, there are many reality check habits that I've built up over time, and one of them is that as I work on my computer, I periodically press my palm down onto the desk to see if it goes through.

So I wrote a handful of sentences and then my palm automatically pressed down on the desk. And went right through it. At that point, I knew I was dreaming, and woke up inside my dream.

When you look through your own life, you will find countless examples of things that you can use or improvise as reality checks. And when you've built up enough habits around that, they will start to happen automatically, both in your waking life and in your dreams.

Hallucinations and safety

There is an important point about reality checks that is often missed. In our dreams, we can experience anything we choose. However, when we hallucinate, this can also be true of the waking world.

For example, earlier I talked about pushing your finger through your palm as a reality check. This obviously won't work in the waking world. What can happen though is that we hallucinate that it did work.

Because this possibility exists, we can never be 100% certain that we are awake, and we can never be 100% certain that we are dreaming.

This has a very important consequence: when we are dreaming, it is of critical importance to not do anything that could cause us or others significant harm if we were to do it when awake.

Let me illustrate by way of example. Suppose that you've decided you want to fly. You do your reality check and discover that you're in a dream.

Unbeknownst to you, you are actually wide awake and hallucinating.

So you climb to the top of a building and jump off expecting to fly.

SPLAT.

Don't do that.

This does not mean that you cannot fly in your dreams. It just means that you have to be a tiny bit careful. Rather than jumping off a tall building, simply take off from the ground.

Similarly, don't run around killing people or driving cars into walls at high speed. If someone is in your dream and you don't want them there, send them away.

It's your dream and you get to choose what happens.

Even if there was no possibility that you were awake and hallucinating, the things that you damage inside your dreams are a part of you.

Meditation and mindfulness

As you can probably guess from the material we've covered so far, the things that we experience in our dreams are to some extent a reflection of the things that we experience in the waking world.

And the sad truth is that most people go through life with blinkers on, constantly thinking about the past or the future, and almost never slowing down and taking the time to be present in the moment.

If we want to become aware inside our dreams, it is important that we first become aware while we are wide awake.

Conveniently there are a number of ways we can achieve this. And it does not have to be a lot of work or consume a lot of time.

In fact, it can be as simple as whenever we have a spare moment, allowing our attention to shift to our experience of that moment for a short while. This can be as short as a few seconds, or as long as the rest of the day.

It all depends on the circumstances at the time.

The way you do this is entirely up to you. I do it by paying attention to all the details of something in my immediate environment and then allowing my awareness to expand out into whatever else is there. You want to make sure that whatever it is that you are focusing on, you do it for a short enough time that there is no possibility that you will become bored.

A few moments of fascinated curiosity about those details is all that is required. Repeated many times throughout the day. Just as with other emotions, when you ramp up your delight in the fascination, the memory is embedded more quickly and easily and you will get there faster.

The important thing is to build the skill of moving from wherever our thoughts were into being present in the moment, so for most people it is more immediately useful to take a few seconds to be fully present, and to do it as often as possible throughout your days.

When we do this, we quickly become practiced at switching to that state. Not only that, but just as happens when we repeatedly conduct our reality checks throughout every day, if we do it often enough, periodically switching to that fully present state becomes an automatic habit. And once it is an automatic habit, it is likely that we'll also do it inside our dreams.

And that leads to us becoming fully aware while we're dreaming.

It won't happen unless you take the time to make it happen though. When you are starting out, you can either add it to the sequence you run through with your reality checks, or set a new series of alarms to let you know when to do it throughout your days. The key is to choose something that will remind you to do it many times throughout each day.

Whether that is by attaching it to something else, such as your reality checks, by setting an alarm, or by any other means is largely immaterial.

Dream journal

So now we have almost all of the tools in place that we need in order to achieve lucidity in our dreams.

Previously I mentioned a lucid dreaming planner and journal, and we've already covered dream planning in an earlier section.

A critical part of lucid dreaming is our ability to recall our dreams. Without this ability, they would be largely pointless since we would forget them as soon as we woke up.

In order to recall our dreams, we need to build a bridge between our dreaming mind and our waking mind.

And the easiest way that I know of to do this is by keeping a dream journal. This is the one thing that allowed me to move from recalling maybe one dream a year if I was lucky, to recalling one or more dreams in vivid detail every single night.

As you can no doubt guess, a dream journal is nothing more than a log of what happened in our dreams.

The way that it works is you leave your journal and a pen beside your bed when you go to sleep at night, and then first thing when you wake up in the morning, you write out what happened in your dreams.

Just as planning your dreams is important, it is also important that you decide the night before that you are going to write in your dream journal when you wake up. And that you then do it.

The way this almost always works for me is that I'll start with just a single thought about the dream when I wake up, I think about it for a few moments, then grab my journal and start writing.

Invariably more details emerge as I write. Sometimes there is just one dream. Sometimes there are as many as three or four.

The longer you set aside to write out your dreams after each sleep period, the more quickly you will get better at this skill.

Our memories work by association, so when we make the attempt to recall the details of our dreams, this causes our minds to automatically bring up other memories around them.

As you are writing out your dream journal each day, make sure that you record not only the people, places and events, but also what you were thinking about and what you were feeling while you were experiencing them.

You see, the only way we can recall our dreams is by going partially back into them. Likewise, the act of writing them out forces us to stay in the waking world. And since our minds are really good at associating stuff with other stuff, the act of holding both the dream world and our waking world in consciousness at the same time results in our minds automatically building a bridge between those two worlds for us.

Once that bridge exists, dream recall becomes easy.

Waking up inside a dream

So now that we've got all the tools in place that we need, how do we actually become lucid inside our dreams?

It turns out that it's quite easy. How you do it depends on the exact method that you use to create the lucid dream in the first place.

There are two broad ways to make this happen. First, you can sleep normally and then realize that you are dreaming when your reality check tells you that you are. And second, you can move directly from being awake into your dream.

Most people find that it is significantly more difficult to achieve the latter, which is why reality checks are so important.

In order to become lucid inside a dream that's already happening, all you really need to do is practice your reality checks throughout the days. Once they become a habit, you will start to do them automatically, and then they will make their way into your dreams.

At that point, you'll find yourself performing a reality check inside a dream because it is just a part of what you do, and suddenly your hand will go through the desk, or whatever other impossible thing you've attempted will work.

Dream stabilization

When your reality check fails and you realize that you are dreaming, the best course of action is to look around your dream and take in all the details. For the first few times that you succeed with this, it is important to do what you can to stabilize the dream so that you don't fall right out of it and wake up.

And the easiest way to stabilize the dream is to pay attention to all of the sensory details. If there is a vivid image, notice all the colors. Sniff the air and discover what you can smell. Touch the various surfaces inside your dream and notice what everything feels like. Pay attention to the textures.

If you've been practicing being mindful during and right after each waking reality check, this should start to happen automatically in your dreams.

The more you can increase your full sensory experience of your dream, the more stable it will become. And as with every other skill you've ever learnt, after you've done it a few times it will start to become automatic. When lucid dreamers do this, eventually you get to the point where you wake up inside a dream, take in the full sensory experience of it, and then proceed to do whatever you want for a few hours, days, weeks or even years.

So that's the easy way. There are quite a few variants of it, and they all come down to turning your reality checks into a habit so that they happen automatically in your dreams.

Getting there directly from being awake

Of course, it's one thing to be able to wake up and become aware inside a dream. It's quite another to be able to go directly into a dream from your waking state.

While most lucid dreamers find moving directly from awake into a dream to be much more difficult, I am including it here because I find it to be much easier to simply transition directly from being awake to being inside a lucid dream.

If you practice daydreaming, visualization, self-hypnosis, meditation or mindfulness regularly, you too may find it easier to move directly from being awake to being fully lucid inside a dream.

There are countless ways that this can be achieved, and the one that I've found to be most effective is to move my attention around various objects of different scales, fully intending to find myself inside my dream. These objects can be anything at all.

When I guide people through this, I will often have them focus their attention on wriggling the fingers or toes on one hand or foot, paying attention to the finer details, temperatures, pressures, tensions and so on. Then I'll have them progressively move their fingers or toes half as much, and half as much again, until they cannot move them at all. Using this method, most people reach what we hypnotists refer to as *Deep Trance* within less than a minute. Then I have them look for a portal and step inside their dream.

When I do it to myself, and with more responsive hypnotic subjects, I will typically take a slightly different approach that has the same underlying mechanism.

As always, start by writing out a plan for your dream and deciding that you're going to have that dream tonight.

After doing this, lie on or in your bed with your eyes closed, and allow your attention to move outwards, listening for the furthest away sounds you can hear, noticing all the details. Try to work out what is causing each sound. After a few moments, move your attention back and focus on the walls around you, getting a sense of everything that's in the room.

Next, pick some object, which can be anything at all. When I do this, it often ends up being a tree or shrub, but you can choose anything you like. Move your attention inside that object and imagine what it is like to experience the world as it. This is usually enough for me to start to zone out quite a bit. You may need to do more or less. The trick is to keep moving your attention between big things and small things, and you will very quickly zone out completely.

Even beginners tend to be fairly zoned out after moving their attention between less than a dozen objects at different scales.

Next, start to look for a pathway of some kind. Sometimes I'll do this by zooming all the way down to an atom and going inside that, while other times I find that a tunnel or pathway opens up in front of me. All you really have to do is keep paying attention and when the pathway opens in front of you, step inside.

Pay attention to the details of the pathway as you travel along it. Travel down that pathway looking for a door or some other kind of portal.

You will know the portal when you find it because you'll be drawn to it.

Before going through the portal, think about the dream that you planned for a moment, and get a sense of what that's like. Then, when you are ready, and you know that you're ready now, smile, and step through that portal into your dream, fully awake and lucid.

Next, just like when you wake up inside a dream, take a few moments to look around and notice all of the full sensory details of your dreamscape.

Colors, smells, textures, sounds. Notice all of it.

And once it seems stable, proceed with whatever it was that you have planned for this dream.

Since you probably don't know which of these methods will work for you, I suggest trying them all out a few times each and discovering which works best for you.

Remember how we can only track four things consciously at once? The key ingredient that makes all of these methods work is the consumption of your four conscious chunks so that you're not messing with the creation of your lucid dream. Each time we move our attention slightly, it consumes another chunk. The countering effect is that our brains also chunk what we're trying to do at the same time, freeing up the chunks we're trying to consume. This means that you may have to cycle through 10, 20 or even 50 different scales, objects, movements of toes, fingers, or whatever else, before you get there.

Luckily this can happen very quickly.

Other methods

There are a lot of other ways to initiate lucid dreams, which I won't go into here in too much detail. The main reason for this is that in practical terms they are all the same.

However, if you have trouble with implementing the methods outlined in this book, you might want to try a method commonly known as *Wake Back to Bed*. In this method, you set an alarm for 5 or 6 hours after you expect to fall asleep, then wake up when the alarm goes off, get up and do some stuff for maybe 20 minutes, and then go back to bed and visualize your dream plan.

After 5 or 6 hours of sleep most people have had all but the last sleep cycle of the night, so if we interrupt the pattern with an alarm and intentionally visualize our dream plan, it becomes more likely that we will experience that dream in our last, and most easily recalled, dream cycle of the night.

A lot of people have reported this method as being effective.

What I don't like about it is that it tends to not be a good idea to interrupt your sleep, so I recommend only trying it if you cannot get the other methods to work for you.

So long as you understand the underlying principles that we are covering in this book, you will be in a good place to create your own methods to step into lucid dreaming.

Shaping your dreams

Now that you've planned your dream and found yourself inside it, next you get to shape that dream.

The key to making this work is to allow it to happen. Do not try to force anything. To see what this might be like, close your eyes for a moment, and get a sense of whatever room you are most familiar with. Notice how and where everything is. That's all you have to do to start to shape a dream reality.

So for example, suppose you are inside your dream and you decide that you'd like to go for a walk along a beach at sunset. All you have to do at that point is allow that beach to take shape inside your mind and you will be teleported there.

See the details inside your mind. Hear the sounds. Smell the smells. Feel the textures and temperatures. Allow your experience to become as vivid and real as possible.

Alternatively, if you have built a reality inside your dream that includes beaches and you know where the beach is, you can walk there, bike there, drive there, fly there, or travel by any other means you might imagine.

Dream analysis

After your dreams, eventually you will wake up. Remember, you can only hold four things in your conscious awareness at once, and if you lose the thread leading back to your dream, it becomes very difficult to retrieve it.

Because it is so easy to lose the thread back to your dreams, it is important that the very first things you do when you wake up are first, think about your dream for a few moments, then second, pick up your journal and pen and write out as many details as you can recall.

As you are thinking about your dream, do not open your eyes, roll over, or move any more than is absolutely necessary. Each of these activities will consume one of your conscious awareness chunks, and you only have four of them in total.

Then, once the dream is clear and you are writing about it, pay attention to where you are inside your dream, what people are there, what kinds of things you do, what kinds of things you are thinking, and what emotions you experience. The aim here is to collect as much information as you possibly can.

When we do this, two things typically happen. First, we tend to become very good at remembering our dreams. And second, since the information has been written down, we can go through it and look for common themes and threads across multiple dreams.

Naturally we cannot look for these threads after just one night. If you recall high school math class, we need around 20 data points for the sample to be statistically significant.

This means that we need to set aside time on a regular basis to go through our dreams and notice what things multiple dreams have in common.

If you've got a copy of my **Lucid Dreaming Planner and Journal**, you'll find a section in the back for dream analysis. If you are using a diary, mark out a few pages at the back for this purpose.

There are any number of ways you can approach this analysis. Whichever way you choose, it is important to set aside time to do this regularly. When I first started recalling dreams, it took me about three weeks to gather enough of them before I could start analysis. Once you have enough dreams to begin, it is probably easiest to set aside a specific time each week when you will perform your dream analysis.

The core of the process is that you read the journal for all of your recent dreams and look for commonalities. You can do this by writing down specific people, places, events, thoughts and emotions in the analysis section at the back of your journal, and then keeping a tally of how many times each occurs. You can also take the approach of reading all of your dreams, making notes in the analysis section. For most people, simply counting each item with tally marks is likely to be easiest.

Now, because our minds are really good at spotting differences, as we read through our journals looking for and noting down commonalities the unusual and odd things tend to pop out quite clearly. When they do, it is important to pay special attention to them as they could be additional signs that you are dreaming.

When you find these unusual things that don't happen in the waking world, perform a reality check while thinking about them. This causes your mind to attach the reality check to the event, so that when it happens inside your future dreams, you will be much more likely to perform a reality check then and there.

In the case of people, places, and so on that commonly occur in your dreams, and are also in your waking life, you might want to develop the habit of performing a reality check whenever they show up.

Think about it: if we habitually conduct reality checks every hour on the hour, we will probably do the same thing in our dreams, which means that on average we will have wasted half an hour of dream time before we realize we are dreaming. Sometimes the dream might even end before we would have conducted a reality check inside it. In contrast, when we deliberately attach reality checks to things that frequently happen inside dreams, this can dramatically increase our chances of becoming lucid. Especially when those things happen early on in our dreams.

If you recall, one of the ways to get things into our minds is by repetition. And this applies on all scales. In the case of lucid dreaming, what we want to get into our mind are just two things: becoming lucid inside our dreams, and recalling them in detail afterwards.

As mentioned earlier, dream journaling effectively forces us to become better at recalling our dreams, since the act of thinking about our dreams while simultaneously writing them down causes our minds to automatically build a bridge between our dream world and the waking world.

And when we later analyse those dream journals and notice common threads and themes amongst dreams that alert us to the fact that we are currently dreaming while fully lucid, our minds automatically attach lucidity to future instances of those threads and themes.

I don't know about you, but my ultimate goal with lucid dreaming is to always become lucid as soon as I am dreaming so that not a moment is wasted! And dream analysis gets us there that much more quickly.

In summary

Congratulations! You've made it almost to the end of this book. If you've followed all the steps, you should be well on your way to your first lucid dream.

We started off this journey by talking about how most people waste a good portion of their lives by being unconscious and unaware for between 6 and 8 hours every night. It is very well known that we need our sleep in order to function, so what's needed is an approach that allows us to become fully aware inside our dreams.

Not only that, but because time works differently in our dreams, once we gain the ability to become lucid inside them, our effective conscious lifetimes can be extended by many years. And getting started is easy and fun!

Next, we talked about exactly what lucid dreaming is. To recap, it is exactly what it sounds like: using simple techniques that have been used throughout all of human history, we can learn to become fully aware and lucid inside our dreams. Once we've done this, we can live out anything we might desire while we are sleeping, and recall it with crystal clarity afterwards.

You learnt that lucid dreaming is a completely safe and natural process, and how we are always dreaming to some extent. All that happens when we sleep is that we lose most of the data feed from the outside world. Just as when we are awake we move between daydreaming and being focused on what we're doing and what's going on around us, when we are asleep, we move through sleep cycles where our brains perform different maintenance tasks for us, finishing up with a dreaming cycle towards the end.

We also covered how we can never be completely certain whether we are awake or dreaming, which has the important consequence that we must never do something in our dreams that might cause harm to us or someone else if we happen to be awake and hallucinating.

Next, we moved on to exactly what to do in order to start recalling your dreams and to start becoming lucid inside them. We went over how our dreams are created by our unconscious minds, and how our unconscious minds are really only good at associating stuff with other stuff, forming representations of objects and abstract concepts inside our minds. These representations are known as chunks.

We covered how the only ways we can really force ourselves to remember things are by either repeating them enough times that our brain decides they are important and should be remembered, and by attaching a large emotion. The larger the emotion we can generate, the less repetition is required.

Using the method of loci, we can exploit our ability to recall things with which we are already very familiar by using those locations inside our mind as a storage facility for things we want to remember. When we do this, we still have to repeat a few times.

All of this together means that if we want to experience things inside our dreams, it is important to first learn to experience them in our day to day life. This applies regardless of whether it is simply being aware of our surroundings, performing reality checks, or anything else. Once we become lucid inside our dreams, we can then take over and shape them in any way we might choose.

A flow-on effect of the way that our memories and minds work is that if we want to dream a specific thing, whether it is for the purposes of studying or learning a new physical skill, or exploring somewhere new, we can hugely increase our chances of doing so by planning our dream before we sleep. We do this by taking a few minutes to write out exactly what we would like to do in our dream that night in our *Lucid Dreaming Planner and Journal*.

Even though what we choose to do is limited only by our imagination, it is important to include the right amount of detail in our plan, and to write the majority of it as something that is happening right now, as this primes our mind to not only shape the dream in the way we'd like, but leaves in the flexibility to be creative. Then we take a few moments to think about that plan in detail before, or even as, we fall asleep.

If we want to experience more time inside our dreams, we can do that by including the amount of time we will spend doing each dream activity in our plan. This is the amount of time that we perceive as having passed, rather than the amount of time in the waking world, so it is possible to spend days, weeks, or even years inside a single dream.

When we want to study, learn a new skill, or even practice physical skills inside our dreams, we can write a dream plan that allows us to create a dream lab that is perfectly suited to us. And when we give this dream lab a name, we can come back to it time and time again in the future.

Since the things that we experience in our dreams are a reflection of our life in the waking world, if we want to become lucid inside our dreams, it is important that we first take steps to become lucid while awake. Most people wander through life in a sort of haze, never really paying attention to the now and always focused on the past or the future. We can learn this skill by integrating mindfulness and meditation into our lives. The key to making this work is to have many tiny instances of each throughout the day. All it takes is whenever we have a spare moment, allowing ourselves to focus on the details of something for a short time. And repeating this often throughout our days.

We can build a bridge between our dream world and our waking world by keeping a dream journal. When we do this, our minds are forced to hold part of the dream state and the waking state at the same time, which causes them to become associated inside our minds. This makes it much easier to recall our dreams.

When we analyse our dreams after having a few of them, we can increase our chances of becoming lucid in future dreams by performing reality checks when we notice things that commonly happen in our dreams and only in our dreams. This attaches the act of performing the reality check to something that only happens in our dreams, which over time leads to us running that reality check when we experience that dream circumstance in the future.

And when we notice specific things from our waking life showing up repeatedly in our dreams, it is a good idea to perform reality checks every time we experience those things, whether they are people, places, events or something else entirely.

Once we have reality checks happening habitually throughout our days, it becomes likely that they will start to happen automatically in our dreams as well. And this leads to us becoming lucid in our dreams when we notice that our reality check fails.

Then we can stabilize our dreams by paying attention to all of the sensory details inside that dream. When we are starting out with lucid dreaming, it's important to do this before anything else because otherwise we might pop out of the dream and wake up.

We can also move directly from being awake into a dream by moving our attention around things in our waking environment, imagining what it would be like to become those things, and moving up and down in size. With a little practice, we can make ourselves as big as the entire universe, or smaller than an atom. Doing this trains our mind to move between these different states and perspectives. And if we then look for a pathway and follow it to some kind of portal, take a moment to think about the dream we planned, and then step through that portal, we will usually find ourselves moving directly into the dream we wanted while still fully lucid.

Once we are inside our dream and we are in control, we can do anything we might choose. The key to making it work is to not force anything, but simply allow our dream to take on the shape we'd like it to have. It also helps if we believe it is possible, and since it's a dream we already know that it is.

If you want to have good lucid dreams, it tends to be sensible to limit your intake of any kinds of stimulants or drugs, since these can significantly mess with your sleep patterns.

That's really all there is to it. All that's left now is to grab or create a *Lucid Dreaming Planner and Journal*, and start planning, recording and analyzing your dreams.

Conclusion

So that brings us to the end of this book. If you'd like to be alerted when I release new material, you can find details on my website over at maxtrance.com. Or at least, you will be able to just as soon as I've managed to get the signup form working.

I'd like to thank you for taking the time to make it to the end of this book. It is my hope that it has helped you to shortcut your own learning process so that you can start lucid dreaming much more quickly.

If you've enjoyed this book, or learnt something from it, I'd really appreciate it if you could post a positive review.

This helps me out no end.

And if you are stuck on something, please feel free to reach out to me using the details on my website maxtrance.com. I enjoy talking with other lucid dreamers and am happy to help get you unstuck. It also helps me to update the book when I can see what parts don't make sense to people, which makes it better for future readers.

Next Steps

If you're like most people, you've probably read through this book and fully intend to implement the things that you've learnt.

But sometimes life gets in the way and we can forget.

Our minds can only track a tiny handful of things at once, and as soon as we exceed that, things start to fall out of our awareness. That's part of the reason we have trouble remembering our dreams in the first place.

So right now, before you do anything else, why not set yourself up for success?

The easy way to do this is to ensure you have your dream planner and journal organized. That way you can leave it beside your bed so that when you go to bed at night, you see it and are reminded.

Simple but effective.

As I've outlined in this book, there are a few options here:

- Use a couple of sheets of paper from your printer.
- Use a diary or notebook.
- Use a proper **Lucid Dreaming Planner and Journal**

Whichever you choose, I recommend organizing it right now. It takes only a few moments to grab some paper or a notebook, or to order your **Lucid Dreaming Planner and Journal** online.

Do this now, and before you know it, you could be having the dreams of your dreams.

Follow Max Trance Online

Facebook Page: fb.me/theMaxTrance

Facebook Messenger: m.me/theMaxTrance

Instagram: ig.me/theMaxTrance

Website: maxtrance.com

Also by Max Trance

Lucid Dreaming Planner and Journal

The Dream Planner and Journal specifically designed to be used with the material in this book that you're reading right now. Available in paperback.

Artful Hypnotic Anchoring

A guide on how to construct and use hypnotic anchors. Available as an eBook and in paperback.

Hypnosis Quick Start Guide

Step by step instructions designed to take you from complete beginner to hypnotizing your first subject. Available as an eBook and in paperback.

Hypnosis Quick Start Workbook

Mostly the same as the Hypnosis Quick Start Guide, only with spaces to write out your answers to the questions I've found to be important to ask when you would like to become good at hypnosis. Available in paperback.

10 More Fun Things to Do With Hypnosis

Additional hypnotic phenomena to use with the processes in the Hypnosis Quick Start books. Available as an eBook from maxtrance.com/10more.

The Quit Smoking Formula

This one is designed to be a complete quit smoking program in book form. Inside you'll find the processes that I use to help smokers quit for life. Only re-organized so that they can be implemented with self-hypnosis. Available as an eBook from maxtrance.com/qsf.

The Self-Hypnosis Formula

Designed to be the quickest possible introduction to self-hypnosis, this short book covers an exact 7 step process that was engineered to guide anyone into deep self-hypnosis and teach them to use it to leap-frog into hypnotic realities, meditation, lucid dreaming, sleep, and more. Available as an eBook and in paperback.

The Two Page Deep Trance Script

Want a script that I've used to quickly guide the most resistant subjects into deep hypnosis? This short script was specifically designed to do just that. Available as an eBook.

Don't Forget the Zombies: The Zombie Apocalypse Hypnosis Script

Want to help your friends to believe they lived through a zombie apocalypse then have them tell you all about it? This book was specifically designed to show you how to do just that. Available as an eBook and in paperback.

Printed in Great Britain
by Amazon